We Alive

with death?life love awakening healing beings'n'being?

A booknbooks maybe

Seb Mjacmbrao

Published in 2020 by We Alive Books

We Alive

ISBN Paperback: 978-1-8380306-0-5

Ebook: 978-1-8380306-1-2

Typesetting and Cover design by: Art Noise - www.artnoise.net

Transcribing: Jodene Antoniou - www.capitalcaptions.com

Proof-editing: Dawn Austin Locke - www.dawnproofperfect.co.uk

A CIP catalogue copy of this book can be found in the British Library.

Published with the help of Indie Authors World

www.indieauthorsworld.com

IndieAuthors World

Seb Mjacmbrao is a member of the Alliance of Independent Authors

...we alive...

CONTENTS

About the Author and maybe the Reader

You'll find out more about me and a We Alive network as you read this book. Each purchase of the book contributes to escalating donations to We Alive Fund (WAF) for all of us and our planet. This is perhaps one way among many that we can collaborate with and be part of the myriad personal, local, global initiatives facing our challenges, helping to foster survival, wellbeing, a better life and world for each of us, now and in the future - and for generations to come.

Acknowledgements

To everyone involved in We Alive — those mentioned on the copyright page and many other people too — I'm so touched by, grateful for the countless different ways you've collaborated with me in helping to bring this into being.
Thanks so much!

What If... in our reading, writing, living and being we're individually yet together on a maybe universal as well as personal quest – sometimes in the midst of pain, suffering and tragedy, while still seeking, exploring, experimenting with language, life and love...

what if there's one myriad alive death?life invitation of love for each of us and anyone to share?... sharing our invitations in our planetary (maybe personal too) crisis – can we survive it and thrive, be alive?...

sharing including through opening ourselves in a dying?living alive experience maybe, here, now – as a book opens with books – as maybe space opens meaning in partnership with words – as punct.u,a?-!t)*/(...i;~o:n maybe opens clarity yet mystery – as the verbal page opens maybe with the visual page – as not-knowing and knowing open maybe together – as time maybe opens...

maybe beings opening with being...

as individually and together we maybe open by myriad

one death?life alive . . .

*

. . . .

maybe open
by myriad one
death?life
alive...
A Maybe
Death?Life
Alive Touch

*

A Maybe Death?Life Alive Touch

*

?...

*

...maybe there exists one myriad touch – a healing touch – touching an agony of potential annihilation, personally and globally, maybe universally –

touching maybe by dying?living alive – touching potential survival and wellbeing with possibility and trust...

*

....

survival
and wellbeing
with possibility
and trust...
A Way Through
Horror Meeting
Healing Maybe?

*

A Way Through Horror Meeting Healing Maybe?

*

. . . ?

*

. . . opening maybe through a healing with horror beyond hope, into hope alive . . .

*

. . . .

a healing
with horror
beyond hope,
into hope
alive…
Love
Maybe

*

Love Maybe

*

...?...

*

...alive engaging maybe with compassion, terror, rage, grief, renewal, courage, care, happiness – maybe unfolding...

*

Once upon a lifetime, maybe an alive death?life love time...

...against though maybe with death(?) a time alive...

*

...with a question as to what my time alive might be...

I began writing a book

. . . except the book kept becoming a lot of books with a lot of titles . . . except these kept becoming one book with one title . . . except the book and the title kept changing . . . except all the books and all the titles kept staying the same . . . except . . .

well – here it now is: one book, one title; containing several books, several titles; with all the books, all the titles in a sense being – the book – the title –

maybe each book and title dying(?)-yet-living through all the others – maybe all alive through each:

a death?life love alive booknbooks maybe

*

. . . .

death?life
love alive
booknbooks
maybe
Maybe A
Wordless Word
Yet Love

*

Maybe A Wordless Word Yet Love

*

Maybe only a wordless word can say it. Yet maybe love does say it. And to help myself heal I maybe also need a compassionate, honest word for everything in me that isn't love, or is against love, or is an absence of love, or an illusion of love:

so maybe a loving word for everything in me that is non-(love) / anti-(love) / void-(love) / delusion-(love) . . .

or abbreviated: n/a/v/d-(love): navd-(love) . . .

maybe I'm living with a mix of navd and love, and maybe there's an alive way through the mix with love . . .

*

. . . .

an alive way
through the mix
with love...
Maybe Love With
Healing

*

Maybe Love With Healing

*

When one day I'm experiencing what we often call 'dying'... at the end(?) of my life with everyone and everything in this world and universe... and if I'm conscious... aware... and not overwhelmed by pain... or maybe chaos... or maybe in another way I can't right now foretell... facing what we often call 'death'... this is what I feel I'll care about... love alive with healing... love...

*

And from my very beginning(?)... as a human being among the other human and living beings and things with me in space and time... facing what we often call 'life'... this, I feel, has been and is what matters most: love with healing anywhere healing is needed – including healing navd... love alive...

*

Love with healing touches maybe within, around and between; whereas navd nontouches, antitouches, delusiontouches – navdtouches – within, around and between: so love and navd seem almost to me like two poles which maybe I have in common with other people as we face death and life – as we seek a way with our living and dying – alive within ourselves and with each other along with the other living beings and things of our planet, of our cosmos . . .

*

Yet at the same time it seems to me that maybe navd and love aren't poles . . . love may hold all, including compassion with navd in healing – whereas navd, at least as I have experienced and witnessed it, appears only to hold navd – bringing unhappiness, pain and suffering, often coming with hurt and harm, sometimes trauma, sometimes addiction, anorexia or other compulsions, sometimes abuse of self, others and life in our world – both active abuse and passive abuse/neglect – causing devastation, culminating at times in death – turning human beings against themselves and one another, against other living beings, against our living planet, endangering the survival of humankind, even Earthkind – threatening to annihilate humanity and our planetary kindred, extinguishing us from the life of our unfolding universe . . . and my question, vulnerability, growing source of strength, hope is whether maybe love can hold even this potentially terminal planetary navd – can gradually maybe create healing of this illness for the survival and wellbeing of our world, touching what is maybe most natural in us: our instinct, need and desire for life . . . and so touching what has maybe always been most natural in us throughout our around four billion years of evolution, in generation upon generation of organisms living and dying since life began on our planet . . . touching what maybe will always be most natural in us – our natural instinct to meet our natural need for survival and follow our natural desire for wellbeing . . . so maybe love can touch and also open a naturally responsive combined instinct, need and desire to do what we can to reduce and limit unhappiness, suffering and any threat of harm or death, in order to protect and increase our survival and wellbeing... so in encountering new challenges to our survival and wellbeing from new threats of harm, suffering and death, maybe love can touch, open and also nurture a naturally resourceful instinct, need and desire to evolve consciously and find new responses to meet the new threats – thereby finding maybe new benefits too, for ourselves and our world... so in our present challenge, amidst planetwide devastation from the illness of navd including self-abuse and abuse, with planetwide threat to ourselves and Earth's billions of years of life – maybe love can touch, open, nurture and also inspire a naturally creative, interdependent, wholistic instinct, need and desire to evolve in our conscious resources to meet this threat – while making opportunities that can bring healing and allow individuals, communities and our world to thrive... so today, maybe love can touch, open, nurture, inspire and also underpin an instinct, need, desire to evolve naturally and consciously in the creative choices we make individually and together as we seek a way with our living and dying – evolve naturally, consciously, into maybe becoming more as we can really be, in the vulnerability and power of our interdependent freedom as individually and together we face death and life . . . maybe ever more naturally, ever more consciously evolve together and individually as we live perhaps growingly in body, heart, mind, spirit and soul from day to day – our past, present and potential future with their billions of years in wholistic life-wisdom touching, opening, nurturing, inspiring, underpinning our healing through our alive experience maybe of love . . .

*

Maybe I – maybe we? – can never pin down or 'know' what love is . . . yet maybe we recognise love by our experience . . . including maybe experiencing ever greater pain the less we experience love, the more we experience the illness of navd . . . and maybe the less we experience love in our lives and the more we experience navd, the less we experience our natural, conscious instincts, needs, desires – therefore the less maybe we experience our natural, conscious wisdom and freedom . . . true for me over the course of my life, starting with less love, more navd, now gradually switching and, it seems to me, gradually becoming less navd, more love – I'm gradually healing from the pain of experiencing toxic, damaging, sometimes life-shattering, unfreedom and unwisdom with misdirected instincts, needs, desires – therefore misdirected choices and actions through which I've navded myself, others and our planet, including at times abusing myself, others, our planet – causing hurt, suffering, harm and nearly death to myself, and at times to other people too, as well as contributing to destruction against our living world of living beings . . . and in a maybe threefold freedom within compassion: I've needed to recognise compassionately and freely that I have an illness – yet freely hold myself compassionately accountable for harming and now making restoration as best I can to myself, others and our world – while compassionately doing what I can to heal and free myself from this illness of navd . . . an illness with me through what is neither whole nor part or is against parts and wholeness – mixing with every area of my life in relationship with myself, others, our world and universe – affecting my body, emotions, mind, perceptions, impulses, behaviours and way of being . . . an illness arising in maybe different ways in different people – in me mainly through damage from my early life and childhood with intergenerational dysfunction, abuse, trauma and compulsion (in all senses); while also arising in me, as I see it, partly through genetic dysevolution, partly through cultural dysevolution, and maybe through other factors too – so an illness which in me combines 'nurture' with 'nature', 'culture' and maybe more... I didn't choose the illness yet with healing I'm gradually experiencing greater choice... and from the beginning of my life I was conceived, wombed, born, reared and educated in the wake of maybe uncountable generations with this illness; I was a forming, gestating, birthing, growing, developing human being – cellular, embryonic, foetal, baby, child, teen – vulnerable, impressionable and dependent on adults with the illness: my parents and others: who as human beings had once, like me, been forming, gestating, birthing, growing, developing, cellular, embryonic, foetal, babies, children, teens, vulnerable, impressionable, dependent on their parents and others with the illness: within compassion they weren't as adults to blame for their suffering and illness – and to a certain degree they gave me care and, I feel, maybe to the degree they could with the illness, love – yet in a freedom within compassion they were also accountable for hurting and harming me with navd including active and passive abuse; and I – like them decades before me – had no choice in my dependence; I was – like them before me – helpless amidst insufficiency maybe of love, amidst this illness – amidst the unhappiness, harm, suffering, trauma, agony and potential for death that I was living with, and witnessing others live with too; I – like them before me – could do nothing about my hurt, my wounds, my distress – my damage and pain . . . yet in my independence as an adult I can do something for this damage and pain through opening myself maybe to the reality of love – and so opening my awareness to the reality of an illness in me, in others, in planetary humanity: in our living world with which we with other living beings interdepend for life . . . opening my freedom in compassion, my feelings and my accountable responding to the reality of the unhappiness, the reality of the harm, the reality of the suffering, and the reality of the death caused by the illness . . . the reality of navd . . . . . . in all its forms . . . . . . navd with self, navd with others, navd with life on Earth . . . . . . individual navd, collective navd . . . . . . active navd (by doing), passive navd (by not doing) . . . . . . inner navd (with self), outer navd (with self, others, the living world) … … conscious navd, unconscious navd … … ranging from subtle navd to extreme navd – from navd that is almost conventional to navd with levels of self-abuse and abuse that shatter any convention of our humanity … … … and in my experience, the illness – the navd – can at times cover pain with an illusion of natural conscious instinct, need and desire – an illusion of choice; freedom; wisdom; power; even love … … … but in reality as I see it, this navd-illness of whatever degree binds people to itself and binds them in pain … … … and maybe the less there is love, the more the navd-illness binds an individual and/or collective in what is neither whole nor part or is against parts and wholeness – mixing with every area of their life in relationship with themselves, others, our world and universe – affecting their body, emotions, mind, perceptions, impulses, behaviours and way of being – bringing them ever greater pain … … … ever greater unfreedom and unwisdom … … … ever greater misdirection of their instincts, needs, desires … … … so ever greater misdirection of their choices and actions … … … as they navd … … … individually and/or collectively … … … actively maybe, passively maybe, in reality maybe both … … … inwardly maybe, outwardly maybe, again in reality maybe both … … … navding themselves maybe, others maybe, the world maybe – in reality maybe all … … … navding anywhere in the range of navd from the most subtle and near-conventional to the most extreme with self-abuse and abuse furthest beyond our conventions of humanity … … … navding consciously and/or unconsciously … … … causing harm and suffering … … … maybe causing death … … … even maybe their own … … … and ultimately the navd-illness of each individual and each collective combines maybe with all other navd-illness … … … ultimately each case of navd-illness maybe adds to the already existing harm and suffering on our planet … … … and ultimately all navd-illness has consequences that sooner or later could lead to the threatened destruction of humankind and the life in our world – and maybe even other worlds and forms of life – from the navd-illness maybe of human beings migrating from Earth and/or from navd-illness maybe among other living beings in the alive cosmos … … …

*

As I live my daily life … … … in this universe … … … on this planet … … … with my co-humans and other Earthkindred … … … from day to day with the consequences and anguish of individual, collective and planetary navd-illness for me, others and our world … … … experiencing this tragedy, experiencing a sometimes overwhelming sense of dread impossibility in living my life, experiencing what can feel like a dying sense of death, there's maybe a way open to me, an alive way maybe shared and travelled with others yet also individual and personal to me or another – a way by which maybe each day I can gradually through what I'm experiencing come to terms with reality, growingly come to compassion and clarity facing the devastating, potentially deadly impact of navd-illness on me, others and our world – come gradually with what I'm experiencing each day into growing trust in love's maybe known unknown power for healing, come into growing hope for me, others and our world, hope for what I can do individually and participating with others – let myself in what I'm experiencing choose in growingly surrendering my being to the maybe unknowingly known power of love, thereby finding courage for what I can do each day both alone and with others towards a healing for me, others and our world… … … and so maybe a daily way… … … never the same yet somehow the same, day by day, situation by situation, moment by moment… … … a way gradually with maybe all the parts and the whole of experiencing being, while living and dying facing death facing life with myself and others on this planet in this cosmos… … … a daily way by which maybe I can seek to live experiencing being parts-and-whole through and with love – live consciously by my natural instinct, need, desire for diverse yet interconnected parts-whole life – do what I can naturally, consciously towards survival and wellbeing for me as an individual and in community with other human beings within the parts-whole community of life on our planet – evolve naturally, consciously in parts-whole life-kindship with myself, others and our living world – so engage with myself and others in natural, conscious, individual and community action towards a gradual parts-whole healing of navd-illness including abuse (inner navd and abuse with self as well as outer with self, others and life on Earth) – play my whole part in a gradual reduction in harm, suffering and death, and the threat of planetary death for our world and maybe others – be part of our whole in a gradual planetary increase in survival, in sustainability and renewal of life, in wellbeing – a gradually growing partness-wholeness maybe, for people individually, for our collective planet-community with our Earthkindred, and for our possible future universe-community with other beings and worlds… … … a daily way by which maybe I can gradually live more and more naturally, more and more consciously, more and more parts-whole, make growingly natural, conscious, parts-whole choices day to day, gradually live growingly with and through love… … … and this daily never-the-same-yet-somehow-the-same way sometimes seems to me clear and sometimes doesn't, since in day-by-day life, love and navd-illness themselves sometimes appear to me to be clear and sometimes don't – at times I have no doubt that something is navd and something else is maybe love; yet at other times navd and love can to me seem to mix maybe, even blur, from moment to moment, situation to situation, in what can appear to be an ever-shifting kaleidoscope of harm and healing; wellbeing and illbeing; even potential death and survival – a multi-dimensional spectrum of my sometimes confusing, even bewildering, at times agonising, possible choices here and now; including somewhere a choice maybe of greatest love, also maybe a choice of greatest navd, as well as choices of all gradations and combinations in between … … … yet this is more than a kaleidoscope or spectrum; maybe inexpressibly more – this is navd-illness and maybe love; the reality of my life; the ground of my existence, and of my values, my dreams; the core of my being, in kindred relationship with myself and with my kindred co-humans, my other Earthkindred, my kindred planet, my kindred cosmos; in each moment, each situation, each choice, each consequence; this is real harm, real suffering; real healing, real survival, real wellbeing; this really is me with everyone and everything; this is life-and-death – not immediately most of the time, yet ultimately all the time maybe – the living and dying of moments, situations, choices: the living and dying of opportunities for healing, for wellbeing, ultimately for survival: the living and dying of myself, others and our life-community alive on Earth and maybe across the universe … … … and in all this I experience and face the reality of living with others as we evolve within billions of years of life through generations living and dying – generations alive evolving, prone to dysevolving too, while evolving biologically, culturally, linguistically, nurturely – generations past, present, potential future – generations with me through my ?beginning conceived in a single cell, through my dying ?end, through my entire life, through this moment now writing this book or booknbooks… … … and so I experience and face the reality of evolving with others within a mix: navd-illness (insufficiency maybe of love) causing unhappiness, suffering and potential for death, mixed with (maybe love) healing for survival and wellbeing… … … and as I experience and face the reality, the pain of individual and collective navd-illness, with its harmful, ultimately deadly dysnurture, dysnature, dysculture, dyslanguage and maybe more, I face the reality and pain of the navd that I and others have suffered, that people including me have caused – the reality, wounding and tragic devastation in the consequences for me, others and our world – including unknown consequences for my and our future, even maybe for other beings in our universe; and with compassion, with passion, I need to do all I can individually and with others towards healing and co-healing the unhappiness, harm and suffering from navd, towards supporting and co-supporting life; also I need to recognise the reality, the pleasure of the positive contributions and co-contributions that I and others have received in life and given in life – the reality, pleasure and reward in individual and shared contributions given and received for the healing, survival, wellbeing of me, others, our world – contributions again creating consequences, including maybe for our possible future community of beings in the universe – I'm gradually with myself, with others embracing these life-contributions and rewards in joy and gratitude, learning little by little to create and co-create further individual and shared life-contributing rewards where I can … … … I'm experiencing the mix of my life shifting gradually … … … from navd-illness through and into healing … … … individual healing touching healing collectively … … … a gradual inner and outer healing of my navd-illness including healing abuse inwardly and outwardly … … … linking as I can with others in the wider healing of navd-illness and abuse in our world … … … including the wider compassionate, passionate fight necessary at times to stop abuse, and the aim wherever possible to create healing for all … … …

the wider heartfelt, aware, accountable action for survival and wellbeing… … … individuals and communities, at times in harmony, at times in conflict, at times in conflict resolution – each seeking a way, alongside others seeking a way, including me seeking a way, a relating and inter(-)relating way, within a global interrelating of a planetary community seeking a way… … … a way combining, I hope, global purpose with individual freedom – a way that in the face of worldwide navd-illness threatening extinction to humanity and even life on Earth, can allow global purpose to emerge and be fulfilled through an interrelating emergence and fulfilment of growing freedom for all… … … and as I live each day, my freedom – my freedom in life – maybe my only real freedom – seems to me a freedom to face the tragedy of my unfreedom from navd-illness, so seek freely to open myself and surrender to love – and seek to practice and live love with courage as best I can with myself, others and life, even while maybe never knowing what love is, yet recognising love gradually maybe in experience: a freedom to maybe seek experiencing of love – in all, with all, through all – including in, with, through the pain when in parts of what I'm experiencing I've felt at times like love doesn't exist, or even if it does exist, like I want nothing to do with it, or even if I want something to do with it, like I don't know how – or even if in some way I maybe have had an idea how, feeling like all the same I've wanted the choice of navd, even abuse with myself, others, our world, despite the inevitable consequences – despite the inevitable unhappiness, harm, suffering, ultimately threat of death for myself, others, even our living community in the cosmos: a freedom maybe still, through what I'm experiencing, to face the tragedy, devastation and agony of what feels like brokenness, unfreedom, danger with navd-illness, and in experiencing growing mistrust of navd with growing trust and hope in healing, freely surrender – entrust myself to love while, as best I can, living love with courage, compassion and integrity with myself, others, our world and universe – and maybe through experiencing love with healing find sensitive strength and guiding discernment, so navigate to the best of my ability through realities and unrealities of love and navd-illness; navigate both with the parts-whole of myself in my inner world-and-universe and with the people, living beings and things parts-whole together with me in the outer world-and-universe; navigate in inner and outer community, through an interrelating world-and-universe of reality – engaging my perspectives with the perspectives of others in individual and collective quest of reality ever-unfolding; navigate both alone and with others through life – on this planet – in this universe – amidst the complexity, the simplicity and the questions; amidst the harm, suffering and death (not all from navd yet so much from navd) and the healing, survival and wellbeing (so much maybe from love); amidst the horror and the beauty, and the ordinary things of day-by-day life; amidst my choices and the choices of others, and the consequences of those choices; and amidst uncertainty sometimes about what in truth causes what; navigate as best I can, knowing and not knowing, situation by situation, moment by moment – experiencing what I experience: my pleasure and my pain, and all the rest of my sensory-feeling-thinking-doing-being experience; my inner-and-outer experiencing being … … … including witnessing others experiencing being … … … and maybe for me and for others all parts of experiencing being are gradually becoming more distinct yet connecting together – interrelating maybe – differentiating and integrating maybe – healing – in a gradually maybe more natural, maybe more conscious, maybe evolving, maybe more parts-whole sense of inner-outer-interrelating-differentiating-integrating-healing, inner-outer-world-and-universe, inner-outer-community-with-individualness – a gradually maybe more parts-whole sense of self, relating, reality, death, life, experiencing and being – and conversely maybe, being, experiencing, life, death, reality, relating and self – whole-part of inner-outer-interrelating-differentiating-integrating-healing-world-universe-individualness-community-evolution maybe… … … billions of years of life… … … past, present, potential future… … … and, here and now, me with life as I write, an individual, separate and alone, yet connected and belonging with others on this planet in this cosmos… … … with my freedom maybe to carry on navigating in surrender, love and courage as best I can… … … sometimes I feel lost, sometimes I feel clear, and often I feel neither one nor the other or both together, somewhere between lostness and clarity, more or less sensing my way… … … seeking my way with living; with the reality that one day I will experience dying; that in parts of my experiencing I sometimes have wanted to die, and I don't want to die; I want to live as alive as I can; and I don't want humankind to die, or the life in our world to die, or the life that may live in other worlds to die; I want life to live on, I want humankind to live on, and including while I'm dying I want to live in growing freedom, growing partness-wholeness, growing caring, growing aliveness... ... ... and sometimes I make mistakes, sometimes I do things well, and often I make a mistake while doing a thing well or do a thing well while making a mistake, in the middle ground of part-mistakes and part-things-well, again more or less sensing my way... ... ... while each day I need to face any navd-illness and navd in me, in my life, in my communities with others, and in our world; I need to accept what I can't do, yet do what I can individually and with others to heal the navd-illness, to stop individual and collective, active and passive, inner and outer, conscious and unconscious navd – with self, others and our world – navd ranging from the most subtle and near-conventional to the most extreme with abuse furthest beyond our conventions of humanity... ... ... also each day I need to recognise the healing in me, in my life, in my communities with others, in our world – again accept what I can't do yet do what I can individually and with others towards further healing for survival and wellbeing … … … as I navigate with maybe being-experiencing-life-death-reality-relating-self-others-inner-outer-interrelating-differentiating-integrating-healing-world-universe-individualness-community-evolution-here-and-now … … … as I navigate seeking love … … … seeking not seeking maybe … … … maybe never finding what love is … … … yet gradually maybe unfindingly finding love (?) facing death facing life, alive … … alive with something maybe individual yet shared with maybe each and all … with which love speaks maybe a wordless word …

*

…………

love
speaks maybe
a wordless word…
Maybe
Without A Story
Yet A
Love Real Story

*

Maybe Without A Story Yet A Love Real Story

*

Maybe without a story there's, with each and all, a story of all the stories that tell it, maybe a love real story. A real story without beginning or end maybe. Yet a real story, too, that in some ways maybe begins before any beginning... and can unfold maybe through healing... ending alive wherever there's maybe no end...

*

....

alive
wherever there's
maybe no end…
Maybe…
Presencing
Love…

*

Maybe . . . Presencing Love . . .

*

maybe presencing love . . . / with . . . ? . . .

. . . .

maybe . . .

. . . ? . . .

*

maybe presencing love . . . / . . . with hatred?

. . . .

maybe . . .
gradually healing the wounds, corrosion, violence and agony in self-hatred and hatred against others – while ending hatred's conscious and unconscious harm – yet compassionately embracing hatred's life-energy / so rehabilitating, integrating and transforming hatred . . . channelling it . . . / turning it away from self and others, away from causing harm . . . / turning

it – against – harm . . . / turning it – into – hatred of harm . . . / including harm from navd, especially abuse . . . / directing hatred without navding self or others – directing hatred passionately, wisely, accountably, not against self and others but towards stopping inner and outer harm, navd, abuse to prevent the suffering and death they cause / and so releasing hatred as a caring down-to-earth yet aspirational resource for healing, survival, wellbeing / and . . . while living and dying, a value of courage in surrender and freedom – alive

. . . ? . . .

*

maybe presencing love . . . / . . . with compassion
. . . .
maybe . . .
compassion that includes the pain, tragedy and suffering in navd-illness / compassion for the navded, especially the abused – in me and others / compassion, too, for the navder including the abuser – in me and others / hatred of the navd and abuse – to

me, others and our world . . . / compassion at one with hatred / . . . to stop inner and outer navd and abuse . . . to heal navd-illness / and beyond navd-illness and navd, compassion at one with all the parts-whole of life – and death / parts-whole compassion for self and others, within dying, within living . . . / courageous surrendering free compassion, alive

. . . ? . . .

*

maybe presencing love . . . / . . . with living

. . . .

maybe . . .

living with my living self / with living human beings / with other living beings / in a living world and universe / living in and with the present . . . / living from and with the past . . . / living towards and with the future . . . / living now . . . / . . . living my living / . . . living my life / living my living life / alive

. . . ? . . .

*

maybe presencing love . . . / . . . with dying

. . . .

maybe . . .
living with dying / living with dying now . . . / my dying towards and with the future – when I'll come to my death . . . / my dying from and with the past – in ongoing death through elapsed life . . . / my dying in and with the present – closer to death moment by moment . . . / the dying throughout life / the dying of myself with the dying of other human beings and dying of other living beings in a dying yet alive world and universe / and when it comes – my own ?end-of-life dying / . . . living my dying . . . in living my living life / living my living dying life . . . against yet with death . . . alive

. . . ? . . .

*

maybe presencing love . . . / . . . with a riddle answering

. . . .

maybe . . .

what brings being and maybe together . . . / what holds being and maybe apart . . . / . . . 'and'. . .

. . . ? . . .

*

maybe presencing love . . . / . . . with 'and'

. . . .

maybe . . .

? . . . and one and myriad and inner and outer and self and others and planet and cosmos and parts and wholeness and . . . ? / . . . what holds *being* and *maybe* apart – what brings *being* and *maybe* together . . . / can I live with yet without 'and'

. . . ? . . .

*

maybe presencing love . . . / . . . with 'but'

. . . .

maybe . . .
? . . . but suffering / . . . but horror / . . . but
meaninglessness / . . . but meaning / . . . but . . . ? /
can I live without yet with 'but'

. . . ? . . .

*

maybe presencing love . . . / . . . with an infinitely
paradoxical impossible possibility
. . . .
maybe . . .
? . . . / with 'and' but without, without 'but' and with /
. . . ? / can I . . .

. . . ? . . .

*

maybe presencing love . . . / . . . with a story
. . . .
maybe . . .
? . . . once upon a time . . . there was life . . . there was

death . . . there was pleasure . . . there was pain . . . there was everything . . . there was nothing . . . ? and there was . . .

. . . ? . . .

*

maybe presencing love . . . / . . . with an ongoing story
. . . .
maybe . . .
? . . . there was self with others and all . . . ? and there was . . .

. . . ? . . .

*

maybe presencing love . . . / . . . with time
. . . .
maybe . . .
? . . . time alive . . . / time passing, not passing . . . spent alone, spent together . . . since the ?beginning, till the ?end . . . ? / time . . .

. . . ? . . .

*

maybe presencing love . . . / . . . with space
. . . .
maybe . . .
? . . . space alive . . . / space with . . . me . . . everyone . . .
everything . . . inner and outer ?end ?beginning . . .
nothing . . . ? / space . . .

. . . ? . . .

*

maybe presencing love . . . / . . . with life
. . . .
maybe . . .
? . . . life / . . . emerging / . . . evolving / . . . organisms
/ . . . animate / life . . .

. . . ? . . .

*

maybe presencing love . . . / . . . with body and being

. . . .

maybe . . .

. . . emerging / . . . evolving / . . . organisms /

. . . animate / . . . body and being through life against

yet with death – dying living alive . . . / . . . until finally a

dead yet organic body . . . and being . . . ?

. . . ? . . .

*

maybe presencing love . . . / . . . with sensing, feeling,

thinking, doing, being

. . . .

maybe . . .

sensing sensory sensation feeling emotion thinking

thought, doing what's to do including not-doing . . .

through life against yet with death – dying living

alive . . . being . . . ?

. . . ? . . .

*

maybe presencing love . . . / . . . with death

. . . .

maybe . . .

. . . death / accepted without acceptance yet with acceptance / death / death . . . ?

. . . ? . . .

*

maybe presencing love . . . / . . . with boredom

. . . . . .

maybe . . .

boredom opening a way through boredom . . .

. . . ? . . .

*

maybe presencing love . . . / . . . with passion

. . . .

maybe . . .

passion opening a way through passion . . .

. . . ? . . .

*

maybe presencing love . . . / . . . with wondering where to go next

. . . .

maybe . . .

shall I do this / shall I do that / shall I do . . . nothing / shall I . . .

. . . ? . . .

*

maybe presencing love . . . / . . . with mind

. . . .

maybe . . .

mind mindful and minding . . .

. . . ? . . .

*

maybe presencing love . . . / . . . with wanting to find answers
. . . .
maybe . . .
accepting they can't all be found / yet searching for them / yet accepting / yet searching . . . / searching accepting

. . . ? . . .

*

maybe presencing love . . . / . . . with the planet
. . . .
maybe . . .
a cry through the world (?) / . . . a cry of despair yet a cry of hope . . . / a cry of caring, of courage, of discerning, of taking action

. . . ? . . .

*

maybe presencing love . . . / . . . with soul

. . . .
maybe . . .
whatever soul can be

. . . ? . . .

*

maybe presencing love . . . / . . . with feeling rage
. . . .
maybe . . .
in a living reality with dying and death, gradually
healing the injuries, shock and devastation often
present in conscious and unconscious rage, while
also stopping the inward and outward damage
that rage sometimes causes – and so rehabilitating,
channelling and embracing rage through caring for
life . . . / including when feeling rage about harm from
navd . . . rage linking with heartful, rational, grounded
vision, responsibility and care stopping inner and outer
navd and abuse without navding self or others . . . /
parts-whole caring rage releasing energy for healing
navd-illness and for the survival and wellbeing of
self, others, our world / . . . rage compassionate,

courageous, surrendering, free, alive

. . . ? . . .

*

maybe presencing love . . . / . . . with peace
. . . .
maybe . . .
peace . . . yet a caring war on harm, navd and abuse / . . . yet peace . . . and healing / peace with an inwardly and outwardly healing war that doesn't navd self or others / peace facing death facing life / death-and-life warrior peace / . . . peace ending navd and healing navd-illness / parts-whole inner and outer peace for living and dying / peace compassionately embracing the wounds, shock, reactivity and agony that can feel like peacelessness yet are being growingly healed into and within peace / caring peace with self, others and our world / peace with being alive

. . . ? . . .

*

maybe presencing love . . . / . . . with the soil
. . . .
maybe . . .
our senses sensing the soil / the sense of our soil
bringing food, bringing life / . . . the sense of our soil
living from the ?dying of life to which it gives birth

. . . ? . . .

*

maybe presencing love . . . / . . . with water
. . . .
maybe . . .
water we drink / water in rivers / water in ground and
atmosphere / water in oceans / water in and of living
things . . . / . . . water for the thirst of the ?dying

. . . ? . . .

*

maybe presencing love . . . / . . . with breathing

. . . .

maybe . . .

? . . . breathing . . . / breathing . . . / breathing . . . / till the last breath . . . / with the last breath . . . ?

. . . ? . . .

*

maybe presencing love . . . / . . . with constancy yet movement

. . . .

maybe . . .

? . . . constancy yet movement in breathing and life / constancy yet movement in body, heart, mind, spirit and soul individually and in community / constancy yet movement in planet, day, night, months, years, seasons, sky, wind, rain, earth, fire, sun, moon, living world(s?), stars, galaxies, darkness and light / constancy yet movement by death?life through inner and outer space alive through the universe / constancy yet movement with dying?living through time alive through life and death . . . ?

. . . ? . . .

*

maybe presencing love . . . / . . . with choosing
. . . .
maybe . . .
choosing courage freely surrendering / choosing . . . /
. . . without choosing / . . . yet choosing . . .

. . . ? . . .

*

maybe presencing love . . . / . . . with heart, guts, need, survival, oxygen, blood, bones, skin, organs, brain, muscle, nerves, senses, cells, fluids, food, excretion, rest, sleep, temperature, stimulus, response, genes, organisms, plants, animals, humans, generations, living, dying, death, life, alive, procreation, parents, conception, clarity, mystery, cell, womb, primal, embryo, nurture, foetus, baby, birth, newborn, parenting, family, protection, care, toddler, growing, child, teenager, adult, lifespan, ages, stages, learning, play, creativity, providing, diversity, exchanging, mutuality, solitude, identity (identities too?), integrity, relating, culture, language, comradeship, conflict, resolving – individuals and communities caring inwardly and outwardly, including caring for suffering while healing navd-illness and stopping navd – passion, wellbeing, wanting, purpose, journey, presence, compassion, fulfilment, personal, local, global, universal

....

maybe . . .

and all the other things said unsaid in those words

. . . ? . . .

*

maybe presencing love . . . / . . . with dependence, independence, interdependence

....

maybe . . .

and all the other things said unsaid in those words

. . . ? . . .

*

maybe presencing love . . . / . . . with authenticity yet appraisal, discovery and evolution

. . . .

maybe . . .

and all the other things in those words unsaid said

. . . ? . . .

*

maybe presencing love . . . / . . . with honesty and empathy in relating with self and others

. . . .

maybe . . .

and all the other things beyond words, in words, unsaid said

. . . ? . . .

*

maybe presencing love . . . / . . . with inner and outer

intimacy

. . . .

maybe . . .

and all the other things in and beyond words, touching touch

. . . ? . . .

*

maybe presencing love . . . / . . . with imagination, aspiration, awe and dreams

. . . .

maybe . . .

touching beyond and in touch . . .

. . . ? . . .

*

maybe presencing love . . . / . . . with freedom

. . . .

maybe . . .

freedom in surrender, compassion, courage and

aliveness… / …even with the many unfreedoms of living and dying / choosing without choosing… yet choosing / …freedom…

…?…

*

maybe presencing love… / …with questions

…….

maybe…

being alive to the question / being alive to a possible answer / being alive to life and death / being alive

…?…

*

maybe presencing love… / …with risk and safety

…….

maybe…

life and death… / balancing risk and safety / …alive

…?…

*

maybe presencing love ... / ... with orientation guiding

....

maybe ...

guiding orientation through life against yet with death while dying living alive and being ...

...?...

*

maybe presencing love ... / ... with not deciding and deciding

....

maybe ...

... which way to go / deciding and not deciding / not deciding and deciding ... / an alive way

...?...

*

maybe presencing love… / …with daily life

…….

maybe…

the daily things / …for survival / …for wellbeing / …for living and dying / …for being alive / the daily things…

…?…

*

maybe presencing love… / …with aloneness and belonging

…….

maybe…

alone belonging

…?…

*

maybe presencing love… / …with personality and beingness

…….

maybe . . .
being a person, inwardly and outwardly, parts and one,
a oneness part, alone belonging, with people, with
living beings, with things-being, all being . . .

. . . ? . . .

*

maybe presencing love . . . / . . . with partnership
. . . .
maybe . . .
part-nership / inner partnership parts-whole with
self and outer partnership parts-whole with other/s –
alone belonging, in pleasure, in pain, in challenges, in
rewards – self-caring and caring / partners . . .

. . . ? . . .

*

maybe presencing love . . . / . . . with friends
. . . .
maybe . . .

in pleasure, in pain, in challenges, in rewards, inner friendship with self and outer friendship with other/s, parts-whole inwardly and outwardly, alone belonging, self-caring and caring / friends . . .

. . . ? . . .

*

maybe presencing love . . . / . . . with those who are not friends

. . . .

maybe . . .

even those who are a danger / even those who would kill . . . / can I see the danger and the threat to life / yet also see the human being / or other living being / even if I have to kill in order to defend my life or the life of others / . . . while self-caringly and caringly doing everything possible not to kill . . . to find another way . . . / . . . and likewise, within myself, can I meet what isn't my friend – can I self-caringly and caringly meet the danger to me, others and our world – within myself . . .

. . . ? . . .

*

maybe presencing love . . . / . . . with feeling terror

. . . .

maybe . . .

like with rage yet very differently, yet in somehow the same way – in a living reality with dying and death, gradually healing the injuries, shock and devastation often present in conscious and unconscious terror, while also stopping the inward and outward damage that terror sometimes causes – and so rehabilitating, channelling and embracing terror through caring for life . . . / including when feeling terror about harm from navd . . . terror linking with heartful, rational, grounded vision, responsibility and care stopping inner and outer navd and abuse without navding self or others . . . / parts-whole caring terror releasing energy for healing navd-illness and for the survival and wellbeing of self, others, our world / . . . terror compassionate, courageous, surrendering, free, alive

. . . ? . . .

*

maybe presencing love ... / ... with desire
....
maybe ...
natural and conscious desire ... / evolving desire ... / aliveness-desire ... / with healing / ... the desire of navd-illness gradually healing into ... / ... naturally and consciously evolving freely alive desire for survival and wellbeing ...

... ? ...

*

maybe presencing love ... / ... with revulsion
....
maybe ...
compassionate revulsion about harm, navd and abuse / caring revulsion gradually healing self-revulsion and revulsion against others / ... alive revulsion evolving naturally and consciously in partnership with desire ... / revulsion freely partnering desire for survival and wellbeing ...

. . . ? . . .

*

maybe presencing love. . . / . . . with trauma, wounding and shame

. . . .

maybe . . .

. . . a gradual healing for those who suffer with trauma, wounding and shame, often victims and survivors of navd with abuse / . . . a gradual healing of aliveness in body, heart, mind, spirit and soul – in individuals and communities . . . / . . . while remembering and honouring the ones who died / . . . as healing and freedom are found for the life of the living . . .

. . . ? . . .

*

maybe presencing love . . . / . . . with protection

. . . .

maybe . . .

protection from hurt, harm and consequent suffering

and/or death / ...including protection from navd with abuse / protecting the victim and also the perpetrator / by enforcement on the perpetrator / ...yet with compassion / seeking to heal navd-illness / ...while hating and stopping abuse / applying necessary force against abuse – taking utmost care wherever possible never to exceed necessity / force for healing, and if necessitating the death of the perpetrator, doing so only to protect the life of the victim / protection, as far as possible, for all / inner and outer protection and freedom with self and others

...?...

*

maybe presencing love... / ...with vigour and gentleness

....

maybe...

gentleness partnering vigour... vigour partnering gentleness... with self, others, our planet, our cosmos... touching... reaching... holding... releasing... caring... / in living and dying... alive...

. . . ? . . .

*

maybe presencing love . . . / . . . with family

. . . .

maybe . . .

family of kid/s, parent/s and kin / family of partners and friends / family of community / family of planet / family of cosmos / . . . inner and outer family with self, with other/s . . . can I with myself and others create and co-create family / . . . including in healing navd-illness and stopping navd / can I co-live and live family aliveness / alone belonging, in pleasure, in pain, in challenges, in rewards, self-caring and caring, parts-whole individually and together, inwardly and outwardly, family . . .

. . . ? . . .

*

maybe presencing love . . . / . . . with home

. . . .

maybe . . .
home of belonging / home of places and things /
home of being with self . . . with others . . . with all . . . /
. . . home of . . . being . . .

. . . ? . . .

*

maybe presencing love . . . / . . . with fun
. . . .
maybe . . .
just for . . . fun / just for . . . healing / just for . . .
survival / just for . . . wellbeing

. . . ? . . .

*

maybe presencing love . . . / . . . with getting serious
. . . .
maybe . . .
getting serious about fun and about being serious . . . /
about healing / about survival / about wellbeing

...?...

*

maybe presencing love... / ...with healing
....
maybe...
healing... / healing... / healing... / healing all that can be healed / ...including navd-illness / ...a gradual inner healing within self / ...a gradual outer healing in the world / inner-outer-healing

...?...

*

maybe presencing love... / ...with killing
....
maybe...
the killing necessary for life / killing where killing is needed / and ending what needs to be ended / ...including gradually killing and ending navd / inner and outer navd / inner-outer-killing-ending

. . . ? . . .

*

maybe presencing love . . . / . . . with creating
. . . .
maybe . . .
interrelating . . . conceiving . . . wombing . . . giving birth to what needs to be born / . . . along with the dying that comes with birth / . . . inner and outer interrelating-conceiving-wombing-birthing . . . / giving inner-outer-birth to aliveness – to living and dying – death and life – being . . .

. . . ? . . .

*

maybe presencing love . . . / . . . with touch
. . . .
maybe . . .
inner touch and outer touch / the touch of beingness / the touch of body / the touch of senses and sensation / the touch of feeling / the touch of

thought / the touch of words, silence, doing and not-doing … connecting … / … depth surface touching inside outside / … being in touch … / … being in inner-outer-touch …

… ? …

*

maybe presencing love … / … with separation
… … .
maybe …
an inner separation of parts within a wholeness of self and outer separation of self as part of a wholeness of all / in touch … yet in separation … / … being in inner-outer-separation …

… ? …

*

maybe presencing love … / … with laughing and crying
… … .

maybe…
an inner and outer laughing and crying / of being in touch yet in separation / of being in separation yet in touch / of being parts and one with self and a oneness part with others and all / a crying and laughing of being… / …inner-outer-being…

…?…

*

maybe presencing love… / …with relating
…….
maybe…
…being with inner… being with outer… / …being with touch… separation… / …being with separation… touch… / …being with whole-parts… parts-whole… / …being with self, others and all… / …being with death and life… / …being with aliveness… / …being-inner-outer-with…

…?…

*

maybe presencing love... / ...with spirit

....

maybe...

...spirit of surrender, wisdom, courage, aliveness and freedom / ...spirit of being... / ...of doing and not-doing... / ...of compassion... / ...of caring... / ...of inner-outer-ing... / ...of living... / ...of dying... / ...of...?

...?...

*

maybe presencing love... / ...with help

....

maybe...

...inner outer help helping helped helper inwardly outwardly...

...?...

*

maybe presencing love... / ...with understanding

. . . .
maybe . . .
. . . understanding so little so much understanding . . .

. . . ? . . .

*

maybe presencing love . . . / . . . with suffering
. . . .
maybe . . .
healing the navd-illness of neglecting suffering and inflicting suffering . . . ending this passive and active navd inwardly and outwardly . . . / . . . the suffering of self and the suffering of others . . . / healing suffering where suffering can be healed / alleviating where healing isn't found / and with all . . . care and compassion . . .

. . . ? . . .

*

maybe presencing love . . . / . . . with frailty and

strength

....

maybe...

frailty and strength meeting freely in compassion /
surrendering, courageous, caring, alive

...?...

*

maybe presencing love... / ...with joy

....

maybe...

joy that doesn't ignore suffering in self, others and our
world / joy freely caring / joy alive...

...?...

*

maybe presencing love... / ...with grief

....

maybe...

grieving all the loss and all the suffering / grieving

for self, others and our world / ... including grieving about navd-illness and navd / grieving life and death, dying and living / healing with grief / being alive and grieving freely

...?...

*

maybe presencing love... / ...with appreciation and gratitude

....

maybe...

gratitude without denying grief / gratitude healing through grief, joy and more / ...with appreciation for self, others, our world, our universe and...?

...?...

*

maybe presencing love... / ...with sensitivity and celebration

....

maybe . . .
sensitive to tragedy and hope alive celebrating

. . . ? . . .

*

maybe presencing love . . . / . . . with tragedy and hope
. . . .
maybe . . .
tragedy and hope meeting in compassionate alive
surrendering and freely courageous caring

. . . ? . . .

*

maybe presencing love . . . / . . . with vulnerability
. . . .
maybe . . .
vulnerability touching aliveness . . . / living and dying
vulnerability . . . / against yet with death: the alive
vulnerability of life . . .

...?...

*

maybe presencing love... / ...with power

....

maybe...

power with vulnerability... in aliveness... / living and dying power... / against yet with death the alive power of life...

...?...

*

maybe presencing love... / ...with surprise, trust, fear, anger, desire, revulsion, wonder, sadness, tranquillity, happiness, feelings, sensings, thinkings, perceivings, choosings, doings, not-doings, lettings-go, gettings, losings, findings, relatings, separatings, endings, beginnings, middlings, inner-outer-ings, outer-inner-ings, connectings, interdependings

....

maybe...

the well of interdependings / a well with fear, anger and sadness / a well with death and suffering… / a well with healing… / …and life / …a well with revulsion and desire / a well with trust, surprise, tranquillity and wonder / living and dying / a well with happiness… / a well with interdependings / …alive…

…?…

*

maybe presencing love… / …with reality and truth
…….
maybe…
…death and life… living and dying… / …self… others… all… / …reality of realities… / …realities of reality… / …truth known unknown… / …truth unknown known… / …alive…

…?…

*

maybe presencing love . . . / . . . with yearning

. . . .

maybe . . .

alive yearning . . .

. . . ? . . .

*

maybe presencing love . . . / . . . with resting

. . . .

maybe . . .

alive resting . . .

. . . ? . . .

*

maybe presencing love . . . / . . . with limitations

. . . .

maybe . . .

. . . remembering no one can do it all . . .

. . . ? . . .

*

maybe presencing love . . . / . . . with possibilities
. . . .
maybe . . .
. . . remembering I can do what I can . . . / . . . an individual . . . / . . . unique alone, belonging together with other individuals – including through creating, just as all individuals create . . . / living and dying, facing death facing life / . . . in living-and-dying-death-and-life-individualness alive . . . / . . . creating with limitations . . . / . . . creating out of possibilities . . . / . . . creating . . .

. . . ? . . .

*

maybe presencing love . . . / . . . with limitations-becoming-possibilities
. . . .
maybe . . .
. . . remembering I can participate in community (communicate and communi*tate*?) with others . . .

/ …unique individuals together alone belonging – including through co-creating… living and dying facing death facing life… in living-and-dying-death-and-life-community interdependently alive… / …co-creating survival and wellbeing… / …while healing navd-illness and stopping navd… / …through creative collaboration… / …and creative dedication towards conflict resolution… / …individuals… in community… / …creatively…

…?…

*

maybe presencing love… / …with giving-receiving
…….
maybe…
…*regiveceiving(?)*… / …sometimes including not-giving and not-receiving as part of giving and receiving… / …in touch… in separation… / …in separation… in touch… / …inner-outer… outer-inner… unique together alone belonging… relating… interrelating… / …self… others… all… / …individuals… community… /

. . . interdependent . . . / . . . creative . . . / . . . alive . . .

. . . ? . . .

*

maybe presencing love . . . / . . . with roots and renewal
. . . .
maybe . . .
living-and-dying-death-and-life-roots-and-renewal, individually and in community, generations inner outer generations, creative, co-creative, *intercreative*, children and adults from womb to old age, communicating, communitating, regiveceiving, unique together alone belonging, alive . . .

. . . ? . . .

*

maybe presencing love . . . / . . . with wisdom
. . . .
maybe . . .
. . . aliveness-wisdom . . .

. . . ? . . .

*

maybe presencing love . . . / . . . with living-and-dying-death-and-life-aliveness

. . . .

maybe . . .

. . . ? . . .

*

maybe presencing love . . . / . . . with pleasure

. . . .

maybe . . .

. . . ? . . .

*

maybe presencing love . . . / . . . with pain

. . . .

maybe . . .

. . . ? . . .

*

maybe presencing love . . . / . . . with pleasure and pain together sometimes

. . . .

maybe . . .

. . . ? . . .

*

maybe presencing love . . . / . . . with evolution

. . . .

maybe . . .

living-and-dying-death-and-life-evolution / of aliveness . . .

. . . ? . . .

*

maybe presencing love . . . / . . . with past, present,

future

....

maybe...

billions of years – time – with evolving aliveness, evolving individualness-community...

...?...

*

maybe presencing love... / ...with here, there, everywhere

....

maybe...

billions of light-years – space – with evolving aliveness, evolving individualness-community...

...?...

*

maybe presencing love... / ...with communication

....

maybe...

zillions of alive connections... in spacetime, through spacetime, beyond spacetime... inner, outer, self, others, all... individualness-community... evolving...

...?...

*

maybe presencing love... / ...with zillions

....

maybe...

evolving zillions-with-one... in and through each and all... evolving one-with-zillions... alive evolving...

...?...

*

maybe presencing love... / ...with evolving partness-wholeness

....

maybe...

partingwholing... inner outer zillions ever more

myriad and unique yet ever more in touch together as one… inner partingwholing self with outer partingwholing all… partingwholing one with myriad… partingwholing…

…?…

*

maybe presencing love… / …with clarity and mystery
…….
maybe…
mysteriously clear clearly mysterious…
partingwholing…

…?…

*

maybe presencing love… / …with chaos and harmony
…….
maybe…

chaos in harmony through chaos with harmony chaos harmony... partingwholing...

...?...

*

maybe presencing love... / ...with experience and experiencing

....

maybe...

experiencing experience experiencing...

partingwholing...

...?...

*

maybe presencing love... / ...with sense

....

maybe...

sense through compassion surrender courage beingness body heart mind spirit soul breathing sensation emotion intuition thought personality

clearly mysterious experiencing chaos experience
harmony experiencing mysteriously clear existingness
nothingness somethingness certain uncertain death
dying living life alive self others all cosmos planet
community individual outer inner separations
connections oneness parts interrelating creatively
collaborating conflicting resolving/unresolved
completing incomplete distinct boundaries openings
emerging growing evolving differentiating integrating
pause meaning memory values dreams intentions
wondering questioning answering not-knowing
half-knowing knowing facing meeting situations daily
practical serious playful aspirational perception sensory
feeling thinking doing being presence instinct reflexes
varying-qualities-of-breathing-with-bodily-comfort-
discomfort-pain-pleasure-and-other-varying-currents-
of-somatic-sensation signals awareness responses
interwoven varying-emotions-happy-frightened-
amazed-angry-humorous-excited-calm-disgusted-
attracted-sad-trusting-curious-doubtful-exuberant-
dismayed-hopeful-and-other-varying-shades-mixes-
blends-of-feeling vulnerability power linking impulses
varying-avenues-of-thought-with-varying-networks-
and-or-tangles-of-confusion-and-or-cognisance

needing wanting discerning varying-range-of-options-yes-and-or-no-and-or-maybe allowing focusing intuiting defining choosing visioning purpose goals inner-outer-varying-actions-and-or-inactions providing receiving resting assimilating evaluating mistakes progress difficulties successes exploring discovering commitment flexibility learning trying not-trying beginning middling ending without-ending without-middling without-beginning flowing grounding flying settling centering journeying presencing inwardly outwardly silent voicing sighing shrieking whispering roaring crying laughing releasing expressing engaging creating relating reality? reality (...) honest intimate accountable passionate empathic self-kinship others-kinship world-kinship universe-kinship inner-outer-body-heart-mind-spirit-soul-kinship solitude communication togetherness language movement stability change stillness ¿truth? truth (...) nurturely subtle potent interdependently unfolding here there everywhere past present future now, gradually and exponentially, growingly giving birth to healing, to survival, to wellbeing, gradually and exponentially, growingly killing navd, preventing harm, offering care including for suffering, offering freedom including with joy, embracing both rare and humdrum moments, with more than can ever be described (…)… true real sense… partingwholing…

…?…

*

maybe presencing love… / …with energy

…….

maybe…

energy energies energy… true real sense energy… partingwholing…

…?…

*

maybe presencing love… / …with matter

…….

maybe…

matter that matters from the very smallest particle to the greatest reaches of body-heart-mind-spirit-soul… down-to-earth-among-the-stars-physical yet through-and-beyond-physical: matter of fact, matter of probability, matter of possibility yet matter of dream reality: within space, within time yet through-and-beyond-spacetime-beyond-and-through… oneness-parts-outer-inner-self-others-all-interrelating-matter… matter of life and death, dying and living, alive… pleasure and pain mattering; harm and suffering mattering; healing, survival and wellbeing mattering… ordinary matters mattering, extraordinary matters mattering, matter matters mattering… true real sense energy matter… partingwholing…

…?…

*

maybe presencing love… / …with nature and consciousness

…….

maybe…

true nature sense energy matter real consciousness…

true consciousness sense energy matter real nature…

partingwholing…

...?...

*

maybe presencing love... / ...with an ordinary miracle

....

maybe...
miraculous ordinary natural conscious aliveness...
evolving... partingwholing...

...?...

*

maybe presencing love... / ...with values and meaning

....

maybe...
meaning with natural conscious values... alive, evolving, partingwholing... values with nature consciousness meaning...

...?...

*

maybe presencing love . . . / . . . with progress and stillness
. . . .
maybe . . .
progress with values, progress with meaning . . .
stillness with values and meaning . . . nature
consciousness alive, evolving, partingwholing . . .
values progress stillness meaning . . .

. . . ? . . .

*

maybe presencing love . . . / . . . with destruction and regeneration
. . . .
maybe . . .
destroying together with regenerating . . . through
natural conscious values progress stillness meaning . . .
including gradually and exponentially, growingly
destroying navd and its consequences in harm,
suffering and death while generating healing, survival

and wellbeing – alive, evolving, partingwholing . . .

. . . ? . . .

*

maybe presencing love . . . / . . . with needing and providing

. . . .

maybe . . .

need meeting provision, provision meeting need . . . vulnerability meeting power, power meeting vulnerability . . . suffering meeting care, care meeting suffering . . . challenge meeting resource, resource meeting challenge . . . individual meeting self meeting community meeting planet meeting cosmos . . . living meeting dying, dying meeting living . . . life meeting against and with meeting death, death meeting against and with meeting life . . . needing providing meeting naturally consciously, alive, evolving, partingwholing . . .

. . . ? . . .

*

maybe presencing love . . . / . . . with a silence, a scream, a murmur, a call, a word, a voice, a song, a sign, an inner outer language through and beyond language . . .

. . . .

maybe . . .

consciousness nature silent screaming murmuring calling wording voicing singing signing languaging inwardly outwardly through and beyond languaging alive evolving partingwholing . . .

. . . ? . . .

x

maybe presencing love . . . / . . . with expression through and beyond expression

. . . .

maybe . . .

alive evolving partingwholing expressing through and beyond expressing naturally consciously alive evolving partingwholing expressing through and beyond expressing consciously naturally alive evolving partingwholing…

…?…

*

maybe presencing love… / …with being becoming
…….
maybe…
individuals and communities being as we are and becoming as we can be, with our world and universe, with all being-becoming naturally consciously alive evolving partingwholing…

…?…

*

maybe presencing love… / …with being-becoming ever more alive
…….
maybe…
aliving… being-becoming ever more alive evolving

partingwholing consciously naturally… aliving…

…?…

*

maybe presencing love… / …with a winning opportunity

…….

maybe…

a healing opportunity… healing the losses and ending the losing from navd-illness and navd… winning against navd… winning beyond navd-illness… inner outer winning… winning individually and together… winning aliving…

…?…

*

maybe presencing love… / …with healing beyond and through healing

…….

maybe…

experiencing healing beyond and through healing
without maybe ever having to fully grasp what it is...
healing-beyond-and-through-healing aliving...

...?...

*

maybe presencing love... / ...with unresolved
resolving
....
maybe...
for example: unresolved resolving in accepting
the dilemma about whether to say 'inner-outer' or
'outer-inner' or both or something beyond either,
maybe not worrying about it too much... maybe just
letting it all be understood naturally-consciously or
consciously-naturally (another one maybe not to worry
about too much)... saying and doing whatever maybe
seems ok in the moment aliving...

...?...

*

maybe presencing love . . . / . . . with mistakes

. . . .

maybe . . .
saying and doing what seems ok in the moment and recognising mistakes if they happen – dealing with mistakes aliving . . .

. . . ? . . .

*

maybe presencing love . . . / . . . with doing things well

. . . .

maybe . . .
dealing with mistakes, dealing with doing things well, dealing with aliving . . .

. . . ? . . .

*

maybe presencing love . . . / . . . with preparation and spontaneity

. . . .

maybe…
preparing to deal with, spontaneously dealing with, aliving…

…?…

*

maybe presencing love… / …with feeling ok and not feeling ok
…….
maybe…
not feeling ok, feeling ok, sometimes mixed, feeling aliving…

…?…

*

maybe presencing love… / …with things making sense and not making sense
…….
maybe…
sensing things not making and making sense, sensing

aliving . . .

. . . ? . . .

*

maybe presencing love . . . / . . . with letting and not letting

. . . .

maybe . . .

letting not letting while letting aliving . . .

. . . ? . . .

*

maybe presencing love . . . / . . . with ever-aliving life-force

. . . .

maybe . . .

a gradual and exponential, growing healing-beyond-and-through-healing of life-force, a gradual and exponential, growing freeing-beyond-and-through-freeing from the bonds of the force of compulsion

– the compulsive death-force from navd-illness… an inner and outer healing of the self-others-world-outer-inner-navd-compulsion that forces a holocaust of unhappiness, harm, suffering, devastation, wounding, shock, agony, trauma and death on the people, living beings and life of our planet… a freeing from the living-death in individual and collective compulsion and its illusion of offering life-force, survival and wellbeing… gradually and exponentially, growingly channelling this misdirected death-force into true living-and-dying-death-and-life-force, without forcing yet with sensitively forceful inner and outer liberation, freely giving real survival, real wellbeing to individuals, communities and our world aliving…

…?…

*

maybe presencing love… / …with justice

…….

maybe…

justice… compassion at one with hatred: hatred of navd, abuse and harm, compassion for the suffering in and from navd-illness: compassion for the navded, especially the abused and harmed, compassion for the navder including the abuser and harmer... justice not of 'guilt' and 'punishment' but of fairness, accountability, enforcement, protection, restoration, prevention, rehabilitation and (limited, if necessary for safety – graduated) liberation... inner and outer justice freeing-beyond-and-through-freeing healing-beyond-and-through-healing aliving...

...?...

*

maybe presencing love... / ...with letting the body-heart-mind-spirit-soul live

....

maybe...

a gradual and exponential, growing healing-beyond-and-through-healing freeing-beyond-and-through-freeing from blame, guilt and shame... a healing and freeing of body-heart-mind-spirit-soul or 'bodysoul'... healing the injuries – the suffering – the brokenness – the attack and self-attack in individual and collective shame, guilt and blame ... ending this inner and outer attack against bodysoul ... ending the anguish, the untruth of anyone being 'to blame', 'guilty', 'shameful', 'less', 'bad'... rehabilitating the individual bodysoul and community bodysoul, wounded, sick from attack and imprisoned living a dying-death-life ... freeing the bodysoul from inner and outer attack by gradually and exponentially, growingly rehabilitating and releasing all the feelings and energies trapped in the untruths as well as agonies of shame, blame and guilt – accepting and embracing all these feelings and energies while healing, transmuting, integrating them in the form of compassionate concern and true rewarding caring – freely – conscious authentic accountable passionate natural caring with self, others and our world – living-and-dying-death-and-life-caring ... caring for bodysoul without attacking self or others, individually or in community – yet individually and in community, gradually and exponentially, growingly attacking individual and collective, active and passive, inner and outer, conscious and unconscious navd from the most subtle and near-conventional to the most extreme and furthest beyond our conventions of humanity... gradually and exponentially, growingly healing the bodysoul from navd-illness – growingly healing-freeing-caring through living-and-dying-death-and-life-aliving… letting the body-heart-mind-spirit-soul – in individuals, communities and our world – live…

…?…

*

maybe presencing love… / …with letting the bodysoul live through bodysoul-living… being-living… 'beingliving'

…….

maybe…

living naturally consciously letting the body-heart-mind-spirit-soul being live… living-and-dying-death-and-life-beingliving…

…?…

*

maybe presencing love… / …with growing trust and

belief

....

maybe...

growingly believing and trusting beingliving

...?...

*

maybe presencing love... / ...with a growing war and conquest

....

maybe...

a growingly caring war on navd inwardly and outwardly, a growingly healing conquest over navd-illness individually and in community, a planetary living-and-dying-death-and-life-war-and-conquest surrendering courageously, freely, growingly beingliving

...?...

*

maybe presencing love . . . / . . . with growing prosperity, enjoyment and fulfilment

. . . .

maybe . . .
growingly prosperous individuals, communities, world with growingly enjoyable inner outer fulfilling beingliving

. . . ? . . .

*

maybe presencing love . . . / . . . with growing humility, growing confidence, growing equality

. . . .

maybe . . .
beingliving growingly with humility, confidence and equality . . . humility letting oneself be one among others, confidence letting oneself be one among others, equality letting oneself be one among others . . . individuals and communities beingliving growingly one among others . . .

. . . ? . . .

*

maybe presencing love . . . / . . . with growing resourcefulness and resilience in even the hardest challenges

. . . .

maybe . . .

beingliving who knows how

. . . ? . . .

*

maybe presencing love . . . / . . . with growing satisfaction and rewards in ordinary life

. . . .

maybe . . .

beingliving who knows what

. . . ? . . .

*

maybe presencing love . . . / . . . with growing

anticipation, surprise, humour and wonder

....

maybe...

beingliving who knows

...?...

*

maybe presencing love... / ...with relaxation, motivation and vitality

....

maybe...

beingliving relaxed beingliving motivated beingliving vitalizing beingliving

...?...

*

maybe presencing love... / ...with inclusion, diversity, respect, collaboration and mutuality

....

maybe...

beingliving inclusively each and all beingliving diversely each and all beingliving respecting each and all beingliving collaborating each and all beingliving mutually each and all beingliving

. . . ? . . .

*

maybe presencing love . . . / . . . with emergence, purpose and inspiration

. . . .

maybe . . .

inspiring emerging purpose beingliving . . . emerging through individuals, emerging through communities, beingliving with individualness-community inspiring purpose . . . alive beingliving inspiring purpose emerging . . .

. . . ? . . .

*

. . . .

alive beingliving
inspiring purpose
emerging…
Maybe
Presencing Love
Without Maybe

*

Maybe Presencing Love Without Maybe

*

. . . with the navded and navder
. . . .
maybe without maybe . . .
unconditionally emerging love . . . with each and all . . .
healing navd-illness and ending navd . . . opening
survival and wellbeing in individuals, communities and
our world . . . in maybe many worlds . . .

. . . ? . . .

*

. . . with humanity, Earthity and cosmity
. . . .
maybe without maybe . . .
being a human being with human beings in the human
race, an Earth being with Earth beings on Earth, a
cosmos being with cosmos beings in a cosmos . . .

unconditionally evolving love being...

...?...

*

...with care

....

maybe without maybe...

care including for suffering, care including with joy, care for wellbeing, care for survival, care tackling and preventing harm and navd, care healing navd-illness – inner and outer care with self, others, our planet, our cosmos and all... care while living and dying... care in life against yet with death... unconditionally partingwholing love alive...

...?...

*

...with transforming

....

maybe without maybe...

caringly transformative unconditionally aliving love . . .
with . . .

. . . ? . . .

*

. . . .

caringly
transformative
unconditionally
aliving love…
with…
Maybe
Without Maybe
Presencing Love
With…

*

Maybe Without Maybe Presencing Love With . . .

*

. . . children

. . . .

all children . . . each child . . . parenting every child including those without their biological parents . . . living-and-dying-death-and-life-parenting of each child's living-and-dying-death-and-life-individualness with living-and-dying-death-and-life-family-and-community . . . ensuring all children have parent-family-community care . . . and protection – especially from abuse (whether active abuse or – neglect – passive) . . . children, parents, families, communities healing navd-illness and stopping navd, creating survival and wellbeing . . . children one child myriad children outer child inner children parent child family children womb child birthing children growing child emerging children community child individual children each child all children . . . with children: presencing unconditionally beingliving natural conscious alive unconditional love

. . . ? . . .

*

. . . all people, all beings, all things

. . . .

all people, all beings, all things in the outer world and universe, maybe many worlds and universes . . . all people, all beings, all things in the inner world and universe, many worlds and universes . . . inner outer all people all beings all things . . . with all people all beings all things presencing unconditionally emerging evolving partingwholing aliving beingliving myriad-with-one and one-with-myriad living-and-dying-death-and-life-unconditional love alive

. . . ? . . .

*

. . . self, others, all

. . . .

presencing love with the selves of self and of others with all… self selves all presencing love… maybe without maybe with maybe (?…maybe without maybe with maybe a story without a story with all the stories with a love real story with each with all with a wordless word with alive presencing love with …?)

*

…………

love with...?)
?...Maybe
Without Maybe
With Maybe...?

*

?...Maybe Without Maybe With Maybe...?

*

I've been writing this perhaps booknbooks/ booksnbook during several years when I've been bedbound with chronic illness and related limitations along with possibilities as a person with other people and living beings in our world. My illness may have been at least partly caused or exacerbated by harm from collective-and-individual navd-illness. Other factors could be involved too. At the time of writing this sentence (the final sentence of the writing, even though not of the book) I'm trying various new treatments – who knows what the future holds. Over these years in bed, I've been writing by dictation – as part of my being alive; this includes doing what I can to recover from or at any rate help myself with my illness so I can live the best possible and longest possible life; while also preparing myself for the possibility that (with or without chronic illness) like any of us I could at some point in the natural course of living and dying come to a level of untreatable, unrelievable extreme suffering – where maybe my very last resort and a choice of love in courage, surrender, freedom and compassion could one day be for me to bring about my death . . . and if not, maybe preparing myself for a time when, unless I have an unforeseen and instantaneous death or die without consciousness, I could at some stage be aware while dying and coming to my death without bringing it about . . . maybe preparing myself for what in a sense it's impossible to prepare myself: life's inevitable eventuality (maybe imminent, maybe far off, maybe . . . whenever . . .) death's inevitable known yet unknown eventuality, preceded in all likelihood by a period, however long or brief, of dying . . . and with maybe preparing myself unpreparably for my dying and death, in some way maybe prepare moment by moment, unpreparably preparably maybe, for living my life – for being to the best of my ability awarely, naturally, caringly alive.

*

Here are some things I've written to help me in living with chronic illness:

*

?. . . Although my life has been changed in many painful ways by illness, at the same time maybe in many ways it's unchanged – it's life as life is, with its reality of death and dying as part of living, and with risk and experience of suffering. 'Well' or 'ill' I need to live in natural reality and consciously care for my health as a living being and human being. . . accepting what I can't do while doing what I can. . . including accepting what I can't do yet doing what I can both alone and with others towards healing navd-illness, towards ending navd within and around me. . . as part of doing what I can for my health as a whole – which includes the health of my communities in overall community with others, linking in with my personal health. I'm a human being among human beings. . . and a living being among living beings. . . alive alone yet alive with others. . . alone and with others in the presence of suffering, dying and death while living life alive.

*

Again alone yet like others I have a lifetime. . . a time

alive . . . past, present and potential future at the age I am right now. My time . . . my time . . . my time . . . (? and before conception? and after death?). . . my time . . . alive.

*

For me as for others time alive (?death?life?) is maybe to a big extent a matter of health and illness – both in the amount of time I may be alive (at least with my body) and in the quality of that time, including actual and potential suffering. And sometimes I've felt anxious about having chronic illness . . . scared . . . even distraught . . . terrified. Sometimes I've felt frustrated . . . angry . . . at times furious – raging inside – unable with illness to truly express my fury physically and vocally. I've had times, too, of sadness and desolation . . . with a sense of loss . . . and moments of anguish and deep grief. And sometimes I've felt these feelings in a mix, and other feelings too, including longing . . . loneliness . . . and shame – though shame has slowly been losing its grip on me as I gradually heal from navd-illness, growingly find more freedom and caring within myself and in community with others. And so when I've felt terror, rage, grief and other painful feelings including shame, I've felt them with growing compassion for myself in my physical, mental and emotional suffering, my struggles and challenges – along with growing compassion, too, for others in theirs – as well as growing appreciation for our individual and shared capacities, resources, gifts and potential . . .

*

. . . and little by little I've been becoming more able to live my life. Able to live . . .

*

. . . my life.

*

My life is . . . life . . . including experiencing, relating, caring, creating and being . . .

*

I'm alive . . .

*

Alive in my body, my breathing... my sensories, my feelings, my thoughts... my actions... my being. Alive with the life within and around me. Alive by existence and relationship... me and other human and living beings, on this planet, in this universe...

*

Alive through experiencing... I experience. I...

*

...

*

...experiencing being...

*

...

*

. . . I've experienced pleasure in life, happiness too, joy, along with pain and suffering that I've sometimes found hard to bear . . . and sometimes I've felt pleasure and pain touching me somehow together . . .

*

. . .

*

. . .

*

. . . I'm living . . .

*

. . .

*

. . .

*

. . .

*

. . . I will die and . . . ?

*

. . .

*

. . .

*

. . .

*

. . . I feel hopelessness yet hope touching me somehow together as I find these words and write them via dictation into a living?dying death?life maybe love alive booknbooks . . .

*

. . .

*

. . .

*

. . .

*

. . . (?life death dying living alive?) . . .

*

. . .

*

...

*

...

*

...hopelessness and hope... somehow together...

*

...

*

...

*

...

*

…touching… me…

*

…

*

…

*

…

*

…I will die and…?

*

…

*

. . .

*

. . .

*

. . . I'm living . . .

*

. . .

*

. . .

*

From my bed, through my windows I can see trees and sometimes birds and squirrels – living beings, plant and animal, that one day will die and . . . ?

*

. . .

*

Yet from my bed I can't . . .

*

. . .

*

. . . touch the trees which touch the squirrels and birds . . .

*

. . . and from my bed I can't touch the window-glass through which I, a living being, see these other living beings in our world of living, including human, beings that one day will die and . . . ?

*

In a way I'm maybe lost around yet open around how *an individual being or community of beings can link sense in all this… and maybe in love there's something that is sense linking… and touch… inwardly, outwardly, myriad and one… caring… aware… passionate… stopping harm and navd… warriorful peaceful… healing and creating… ordinary yet wondrous… growingly letting go, growingly embracing, growingly freeing… alive… compassionate… grieving and joyful somehow together… intimate… beings… love… being…?*

*

………..

intimate…
beings…
love…
being…?
?…Touching
Maybe
…?…
Maybe
Homing…?

*

?... Touching Maybe ...?... Maybe Homing...?

*

Being bedbound I couldn't go and see my father when he was dying. Over the phone I spoke a poem to him...

a touch maybe / through and beyond space and time / a touch maybe / through and beyond separation / maybe an inner and outer touch / a touch maybe in memory yet present / a touch maybe into the unknown / a touch maybe – of love / maybe love holding releasing being beyond and through / maybe a touch

At my father's funeral the poem was read by a cousin of mine, one of my father's brother's children.

*

And near the end of my mother's life when she was bedbound and close to dying, again over the phone I spoke a poem to her...

although we can't meet / maybe somehow we're meeting / touching maybe through far horizons / so close... / one myriad love – beings being myriad one?

Again at my mother's funeral this poem was read by a cousin of mine, one of my mother's sister's children.

*

Linked with these two poems I was one day thinking about my sibs and extended family, friends... me and my relationships in community with others... me and others who one day will die, maybe pass away, yet in away/a way maybe not away...? So another poem for me and others...

in a way I'm on my own / in a way I'm with each and all of you / a way maybe in touch / touching maybe one and all / a touch maybe – of love / love touching maybe through and beyond space-time-life-death beyond and through / one myriad love – each of us, everyone, everything, our planet, our universe/s...? healing beings with myriad one being?

*

And as I write, as you read, among others in our world...

?...each and all of us maybe one myriad with our inner outer individualness-communities ?touching ?homing individualness-community maybe myriad one, with all and each of us ~ maybe in a kind of unfolding ~ in a way maybe each of us on our own in a way maybe all of us together, a way maybe in touch inwardly outwardly touching a touch of love ...?... love touching maybe reality suffering caring healing homing creation life death dying living alive down-to-earth~presence in with space time truth nurturing body heart mind spirit soul journeying dreams-mystery~presence through beyond space time life death dying living alive~presencing maybe one myriad love inner outer individualness partnership family friendship community everyone everything our planet our universe~s? beings growingly tackling harm growingly ending navd growingly healing navd-illness growingly caring creating presencing homing touching through with myriad one being...? maybe with, through and of love… … inner outer beings being… … meeting… … while meeting pleasure, pain, needs, desires, possibilities, dreams… … …

*

………..

meeting
pleasure, pain,
needs, desires,
possibilities,
dreams

… … …

Maybe… … …
May… …
Be…

*

Maybe… … … May… … Be…

Cosmos… … … planet… … … communities… … … individuals… … … all of us… … … as I write these words… … … as you read these words… … … each human being and each living being and each thing (being a being too? including artificial yet maybe potentially evolvingly real true alive complementary intelligence/ro/bot being?) and… … …

… … …the interconnecting planetwide navd-illness causing unhappiness, suffering and death to our global community of life… … … destroying inner and outer wellbeing… … … killing aliveness… … … threatening the survival of humanity and our Earthkindred – and maybe Universekindred still unknown to us; kindred not by genetic kinship yet maybe life-kinship… … … being-kinship… … … maybe with their own navd-illness, like ours threatening maybe us as well as them… … … navd-illness anywhere it may be… … … threatening the life in our cosmos … … … the life alive in our world, maybe many worlds – maybe many universes, even a multiverse … … … life alive in all of us … … … each of us … … … and within life, navd-illness threatening maybe each and all, no matter who or where we are … … threatening us with harm, suffering and death … and extinction, forever

maybe … … … a way alive … … … may … … be …

… … … a way through navd-illness with love

… … … a way exploring opening unfolding presencing homing touching healing

… … … a natural conscious creative way

… … … a way with survival and wellbeing

… … … a way while living and dying

… … … a compassionate passionate way of care including for suffering

… … …a vulnerable powerful way

… … …a way facing death facing life alive

… … …a way growingly letting go, growingly embracing, growingly freeing

… … …a growingly parts-whole wholistic way

… … …a way with inner outer individualness partnership family friendship community

… … …a true real way

… … …a way here there everywhere past present future now

… … …a way experiencing being becoming

… … …a way with body, heart, mind, spirit and soul

… … …a fulfilling way

… … …a willing way of will yet surrender

… … …a trustworthy interdependent way

… … …a way with the selves of self and of others with all

… … …ways maybe… … … in a way… … … ways… a way

?…

maybe… … … self selves all growingly parts-whole, growingly freeing, growingly embracing inner outer individualness partnership family friendship community, growingly letting go while living and dying creatively wholisticly interdependently facing death facing life, here there everywhere past present future now, body, heart, mind, spirit, soul, compassionately passionately finding ways and a way through navd-illness, exploring opening unfolding presencing homing touching healing, with natural conscious trustworthy survival and wellbeing, with caring including for suffering, with willing will through surrendering, vulnerably, powerfully, fulfillingly really truly alive experiencing becoming being with love… … … may… … be…

…?…

maybe… … … love with healing… … … may… … be…

…?

maybe… … one myriad love healing beings with myriad one being…

(…)

…maybe interbeing healing interbeings loving interbeing~s

(?)

lovebeings~lovebeing?

(…(?(

…)

?)

) maybe with a loving healing touch – touching a human and planetary, maybe universal, abyss of possible utter destruction, touching maybe by life?death dying?living alive, touching a human and planetary, maybe universal, gift for creative healing, renewing and thriving . . . maybe in and through love presencing, while also facing what isn't love, or is against love, or is an absence of love, or an illusion of love: facing non-(love) / anti-(love) / void-(love) / delusion-(love): facing navd and navd-illness – while facing love... facing within and facing out in our world and cosmos . . . facing a mix of navd and love while seeking an alive way through the mix with love . . . experiencing self, others, inner and outer relationship, life . . . experiencing becoming being with pleasure and pain, sometimes both together, experiencing becoming being with the horrifying, the humdrum and the beautiful . . . a personal journey of presencing yet maybe also a shared journey of presencing . . . my journey of presencing touching maybe your journey of presencing touching maybe everyone's journeys of presencing interweaving touching a presencing journey of each and all of us . . .

maybe growingly with self, growingly with others . . .
. . . growingly rewardingly courageously meeting our personal, local, global, maybe universal, challenges of tragedy yet hope and daily life . . . . . . individuals and communities – growingly vulnerably powerfully interdependent – tackling and preventing harm, needless death and active/passive abuse – creating wholistic humane citizenship, justice and culture/s – caring, inwardly and outwardly, near and far, especially for the suffering, and in seeking to resolve conflicts – protecting, sustaining and renewing survival – serious, playful, dedicated, imperfect, wonderful – maybe growingly fostering alive inner and outer security, wellbeing and fulfilment . . . . . .

planet . . . . universe(s?) . . . . maybe growingly with one myriad living?dying death?life alive healing myriad one . . . . and we everyday people, maybe growingly healer-magician-warrior-nurturers, bit by bit steadily ending navd, healing navd-illness, defending and liberating while adventuring in wisdom, wild yet homing – sometimes maybe confused, even feeling lost, yet maybe with increasing compassion and clarity embracing and channelling fear, anger and sadness while harvesting and embracing increasing happiness… … … ordinary extraordinary human and other beings… … … separately connectedly growingly maybe awakening in more and more lovely and loving freedom, passion, questioning, unresolved resolving, complexity, simplicity, balance, joy, meaning and peace… … … one myriad love maybe really being truly becoming – beings growingly loving being myriad one – may – be – unconditional love… … … lovebeingsnbeing-lovebeingnbeings yet a wordless word, without a story yet a story of stories, with realities within reality, with mysteries within mystery, with truths within truth… … … waysnway-waynways… … … sometimes agonising and seemingly directionless, purposeless, meaningless, impossible yet somehow possible and with meaning, purpose, direction, surprising… … … maybe we surprising ourselves – unfolding – creating – differing – belonging – presencing… … … surrendering freely, courageously, compassionately while consciously participating in loving well enough – loving self, others, our world and universe well enough – growingly naturally loving well enough . . . . growingly dissolving and transmuting energies of navd and navd-illness through and into energies of healing and love . . . . growingly embracing and rehabilitating the parts and whole of the navd-ill navd-tortured navd-numbed navd-distorted navd-imprisoned navdself through and within the parts and whole of the growingly healing, growingly relieved, growingly alive, growingly true, growingly free, growingly loving self in inner and outer community . . . . increasingly stopping inner and outer navd with self, others, our planet and cosmos through increasingly sensing, minding, feeling, experiencing, living loving . . . . opening maybe way better sense, way better mind, way better feeling, way better experience, way better life, maybe way to go! ways to be? maybe be may – ways through, with, beyond, by, in a way . . . . maybe our personal yet interrelating ways way . . . . maybe dreaming, practical, kind, determined, flexible, ethical, curious, creative, making mistakes, making better, individual, collaborative, listening, saying, conversing, exchanging, doing/notdoing – being/s – intimate, burgeoning . . . . maybe embracing life?death dying?living alive through and with loving… … … touching joy, touching suffering, touching caring, touching freeing, touching healing, touching body, heart, mind, spirit, soul, touching the selves of self and of others with all, touching-life-?-dying-?-death-?-living-alive-self-selves-all… … so alive, so awakening… maybe maybeing – maybeing love – each of us uniquely with all of us sharingly?…

including maybe sharing We Alive Fund
for all of us and our planet

We Alive Fund contributes to stopping navd and healing navd-illness - it aims for love. It especially funds projects preventing and healing trauma, abuse and neglect of self, others, our planet and world - projects to survive, thrive, be alive.

We Alive Fund affirms that in facing how we could potentially be doomed, we can shape destiny, turn doom around, transform it into life.

We Alive Fund trusts that in our interconnected world, any well directed help, wherever the need, helps all of us.

The more this book is purchased, the higher the percentage of profit for WAF as each sales threshold is crossed:

Sales threshold crossed (number of books sold)	Share of profit given to WAF
1	20%
10,000	30%
100,000	40%
500,000	50%
1,000,000	60%
2,500,000	70%
5,000,000	80%
7,500,000	90%
10,000,000	95%
50,000,000	97%
100,000,000 and above	99%

After I ?die/pass 100%

plus my will money

plus ongoing and future donations

We Alive Fund is linked with a We Alive network of people who resonate with this book. You can meet and get to know them at https://we-alive.mn.co/landing?space_id=1904668.

Because of my limitations with chronic illness, I'm not currently active in this We Alive network. It's other people's baby - growing and developing. I love following its progress and hope to become more involved if my physical health improves. Similarly I don't administer We Alive Fund although, again, I love following it and hope to become more involved when I can.

We Alive is one initiative among/linking with so, so, so many creative, resourceful, wonderful initiatives all round the planet, through which we can help ourselves, each other, all of us, and together maybe save our world?

Milton Keynes UK
Ingram Content Group UK Ltd.
UKHW010010190124
436278UK00004B/383

9 781838 030605